The British Galleries
1500 – 1900

A Guide Book

Dinah Winch

V&A Publications

The British Galleries 1500–1900

The new British Galleries display the V&A's unrivalled collection of British design and art from the Tudor period to the Victorian era. The galleries contain an amazing wealth of objects from Wedgwood vases and Victorian pressed glass, sixteenth century tapestries and eighteenth century wallpaper, to Elizabethan portrait miniatures and Victorian photographs. Most of the objects were made in Britain, but since British design and art has been so influenced by trade with other countries, the galleries also include Chinese porcelain, Italian glass, Japanese prints, Indian textiles and other imports which have been prized by the British over the centuries.

The V&A was founded in 1852 to stimulate British designers and manufacturers, as well as the wider public, by giving them access to great works of art and examples of the very finest design, both historic and contemporary. Many of the objects on display are therefore exceptional, rather than everyday. They were made for the wealthy and privileged, such as the monarchs,

Embroidery from Stoke Edith, Herefordshire, silk and wool on canvas, 1710–20.
T.568-1996. **Gallery 54**

aristocrats, collectors, industrialists and designers who defined what was considered to be beautiful and fashionable. But although the British Galleries contain mostly 'high design' items there are also many objects in the displays that are typical of the goods widely available to middle class people.

In 1500, when the galleries begin, British design and art was not highly thought of in other countries, but by the nineteenth century it was widely admired and copied around the world. The British Galleries tell the story of this evolution.

Britain is taken to mean the territory of Great Britain, in other words England, Scotland and Wales, but not Ireland. The galleries are arranged chronologically though they can, of course, be enjoyed in any order and be entered at many points. The story starts in Gallery 58 with displays about Renaissance style and the court of Henry VIII in the early sixteenth century. It continues through two floors of the museum to end in Gallery 125 with displays on the Arts and Crafts movement and the Scottish School at the end of the nineteenth century.

The displays in the British Galleries have been arranged according to four themes:

- **Style** How things looked, in terms of their form and decoration.
- **Who Led Taste?** The people or institutions that shaped and influenced design.
- **Fashionable Living** How new habits and lifestyles went hand in hand with changes in design.
- **What Was New?** Innovative objects, designs and manufacturing techniques.

There are also five historic interiors which visitors can walk into:

- A room from the 'Old Palace' at **Bromley-by-Bow** from the early seventeenth century.
- The drawing room from a house at **11 Henrietta Street** in London as it would have looked in the late 1740s.
- The **Norfolk House Music Room** dating from 1756 which was part of a lavish suite of entertainment rooms and is now used for concerts and other performances.

- A room in the Gothic Revival style of the 1780s from **Lee Priory** in Kent.
- A late Victorian room from **The Grove** at Harborne, Birmingham.

There are interactive **Style Guides** in the galleries to help you identify characteristic shapes or motifs. Other interactive computer programmes enable you to explore a painting or date a design, and there are also short videos and audio programmes, including music and commentaries on selected objects. Throughout the galleries there are facsimile books and things to touch and handle.

There are also:

- **2 Film Rooms** showing a continuous programme of short films about British design and art.
- **2 Study Areas** where you can find out more about the objects on display. These have books about British design and art and offer access to interactive programmes, including British Galleries Online which contains information about every object on display.
- **3 Discovery Areas** with a range of activities, such as drawing and construction, investigating mystery objects and trying on replica costume.

How to use this guide

This guide highlights some of the most famous objects in the Museum – the Great Bed of Ware, Roubiliac's statue of Handel and George Gilbert Scott's model for the Albert Memorial – and introduces less well known and perhaps unexpected things, some of which are being shown for the first time.

Each section in the book relates to a particular display in the British Galleries and is illustrated by an object chosen from that display. The objects are numbered on the gallery plan on pages 4–5 and events that relate to them are indicated on the timeline on pages 60–63.

The British Galleries (level two) 1500–1760

The maps will help you find your way around. They show only the British Galleries, which are on two floors of the museum, level two and level four. Detailed maps of the whole museum, including all facilities, are available free from the Information Desks. For further help, please ask any member of the Museum staff.

There are also orientation panels, including maps, at the entrances to the British Galleries.

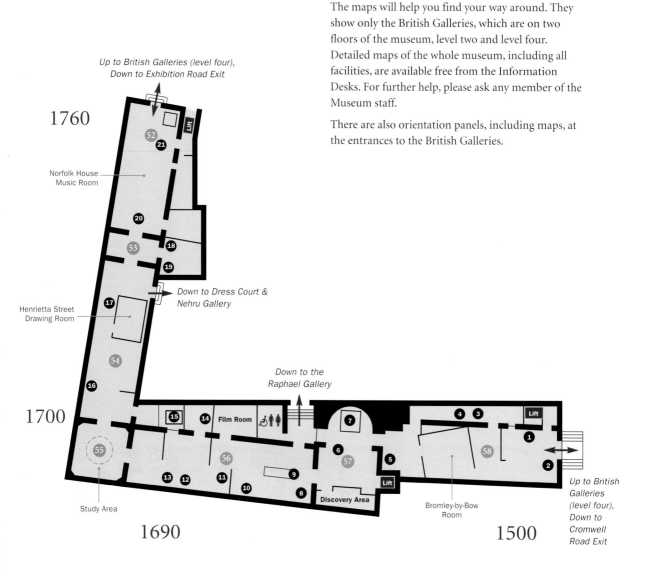

1760

Up to British Galleries (level four), Down to Exhibition Road Exit

Norfolk House Music Room

Henrietta Street Drawing Room

Down to Dress Court & Nehru Gallery

Down to the Raphael Gallery

1700

Film Room

Study Area

Discovery Area

Bromley-by-Bow Room

1690

1500

Up to British Galleries (level four), Down to Cromwell Road Exit

The British Galleries (level four) 1760–1900

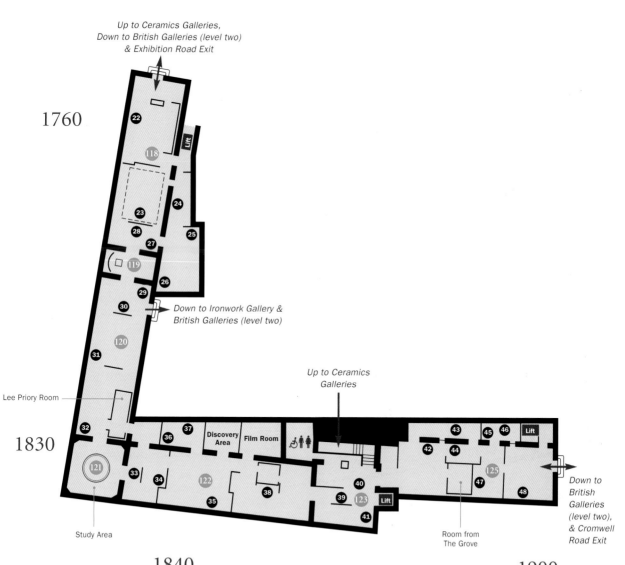

Up to Ceramics Galleries,
Down to British Galleries (level two)
& Exhibition Road Exit

1760

22

118

Lift

23

24

28

25

27

119

26

29

30

Down to Ironwork Gallery &
British Galleries (level two)

120

31

Lee Priory Room

Up to Ceramics
Galleries

1830

32

37

36

Discovery
Area

Film Room

43

45

46

Lift

42

44

121

33

34

122

38

125

35

40

47

48

39

123

Lift

41

Study Area

1840

Room from
The Grove

Down to
British
Galleries
(level two),
& Cromwell
Road Exit

1900

Historical Introduction

At the beginning of our period, 1500, Britain as a nation did not exist. England, Wales and Scotland – which now form Great Britain – were separate countries, and none of them was considered to be a place of particular artistic importance. It was the great European cities like Venice and Florence, Antwerp and Paris, rather than London or Edinburgh that dominated western art.

Four centuries later, in Queen Victoria's reign, everything had changed. Britain was considered to be the 'workshop of the world', a centre of manufacturing and artistic creativity. London was rivalled only by Paris as an international centre of art and culture and British artists, designers and makers were admired and copied throughout the world.

How did this transformation happen? Between 1536 and 1707 England, Wales and Scotland were unified under one parliament in London. In the sixteenth century the economies of these countries were largely rural and the production of goods was relatively small-scale. Over the eighteenth and nineteenth centuries, with the expansion of agriculture and industry, the economy grew and was transformed by new machinery and innovation in manufacturing techniques. This process went hand in hand with improvements in transport and the growth of towns and cities. The population increased dramatically, from no more than 3 million in 1500 to 37 million in 1900.

Britain was also profoundly influenced by trade with the outside world. In the sixteenth and seventeenth centuries its main trading partners were European, but over the centuries there was a gradual increase in commerce with the rest of the world. In 1492 Columbus landed in the Americas and in 1498 Vasco da Gama reached India by sea. The world was transformed for Europeans by these discoveries and new materials, objects and designs had a profound influence on British art and design. Even goods made in Britain were dependent on raw materials such as gold, precious stones, silk and dyestuffs imported from the Americas, Asia and Africa. Britain evolved from a country importing a large proportion of the high design goods

it consumed in 1500 to one that by the nineteenth century not only produced most of its own but also exported them. By the 1850s Britain made close to half the manufactured goods that were traded around the world. The search for profit, resources and new markets for goods was the driving force behind the expansion of the British Empire.

Throughout the period there were also great changes in the structure of British society, particularly with the growth of the middle classes. In 1771 Tobias Smollett in his novel *Humphrey Clinker* commented disapprovingly on how the trappings of wealth and elegant living that had once been the preserve of the nobility were spreading down through the social ranks. He observed that 'every trader in any degree of credit, every broker and every attorney, maintains a couple of foot-men … he has his own town-house, and his country house…. His wife and daughters appear in the richest stuffs, bespangled with diamonds. They frequent the court, the opera, the theatre, and the masquerade. They hold assemblies at their own houses; they make sumptuous entertainments.' This process continued into the nineteenth century. As more people could afford to buy luxury goods, the domestic market expanded and manufacturers made objects for every taste and pocket. Though society remained profoundly unequal, all social classes, except the very poorest, enjoyed access to a wider array of material goods.

The story of decorative art and design in Britain in this period is told in the galleries through four themes: Style, Who Led Taste?, Fashionable Living and What Was New? Together these capture the sheer scale and excitement of the transformation that took place between 1500 and 1900.

The Music Room from Norfolk House, London, 1748–56. W.70–1938. **Gallery 52**

Style

Style is the name given to particular forms and decorative motifs chosen for buildings, interiors and objects. At the heart of the story of British design is the development of classicism. This was the style of the architecture and ornament of ancient Greece and Rome as it was rediscovered and reused during the Italian Renaissance from the fourteenth century. Classicism slowly became absorbed into British design from around 1530, and was constantly used and re-interpreted in the following centuries. The triumph of a very British classicism in the early eighteenth century (Palladianism) soon provoked a strong reaction. By the middle of the century more colourful and exuberant styles such as Rococo and Chinoiserie became popular as an antidote to the cool clarity of classicism, though various forms of the classical style continued to dominate British art and design until the early nine-teenth century. Classicism was partially rejected in the Victorian period when designers and artists experi-mented with a whole range of stylistic alternatives. These ranged from historical revival styles, such as Gothic, to the more recognisably modern aesthetic that emerged from the Arts and Crafts movement and the Scottish School in the last decades of the nineteenth century.

**Style: The Scottish School
1885–1915**
Chair, designed by Charles Rennie Mackintosh in 1897, probably made about 1900, oak with modern upholstery. Circ.130-1958. **Gallery 125**

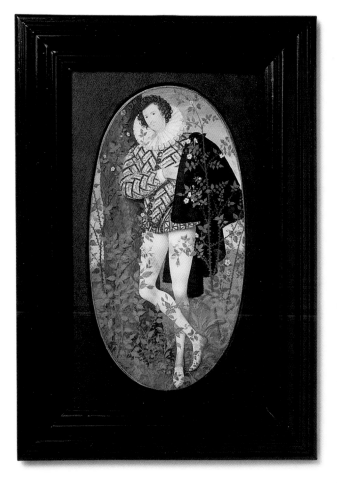

**Who Led Taste? The Court of
Elizabeth I, 1558–1603**

A Young Man among Roses, portrait
miniature by Nicholas Hilliard,
watercolour on vellum, about 1587.
P.163-1910. **Gallery 57**

Who Led Taste?

Interwoven with the history of style is the history of taste. This is the story of the people and institutions that had the power to shape prevailing ideas of what was beautiful and desirable. The centuries from 1500 to 1900 saw various shifts in the sources of this aesthetic authority. At the beginning of our period the monarch, the church and the men and women of the nobility were the leaders of taste. They were the people with the resources to build the largest buildings, commission the finest artists and craftspeople to furnish them and employ the servants to maintain them. Gradually from the eighteenth century influential private patrons were no longer necessarily nobles. Instead a wider range of people and institutions increasingly influenced style and taste. These included critics, professional designers, manufacturers, retailers, and cultural institutions such as museums, design schools and public exhibitions. The galleries trace these shifts through the objects used and promoted by the leaders of taste: from miniatures at the court of Elizabeth I, through the published designs of Thomas Chippendale, to the increasingly sophisticated advertising techniques of the nineteenth century, which include the extraordinary objects made for the Great Exhibition and the colourful posters of the 1890s.

A MILLENERS SHOP.
M.rs Monopolize, the Butchers Wife, Purchasing a Modern Head Dress.
Pub.d April 9.o 1772 by W. Humphrey S.t Martins Lane.

**Fashionable Living: Marketing
Art and Design 1800–1830**
A Milleners Shop, glass print, 1772.
E.620-1997. **Gallery 120**

Fashionable Living

The other element of the history of taste developed in the new galleries is the story of how 'high design' objects changed the ways that British people lived; and how, in turn, changes in lifestyle led to demand for new sorts of objects. In 1577 the Essex clergyman William Harrison remarked that farmers had 'learned also to garnish their cupboards with plate, their joint beds with tapestry and silk hangings' like the nobility. But even these trappings of wealth were essentially functional, for in the sixteenth century very few objects were owned simply for their decorative value. By 1700 this had changed and wealthy people owned objects that were more ornamental than functional. During the eighteenth and nineteenth centuries collecting grew as a pursuit of the nobility and increasingly of the middle classes too. By the Victorian period even the homes of the lower middle and working classes typically contained a front parlour decorated with family mementoes, treasured ornaments and commemorative objects. There was also a parallel process of progressive refinement in both domestic and public life, with the spread of new and often more demanding standards of behaviour, such as the etiquette demanded for dining, or codes of dress for walking, entertaining or mourning. Almost every manifestation of this process entailed the use and display of highly decorated objects and was accompanied by the growth of shopping as a leisure activity.

What Was New?

Between 1500 and 1900 there was an explosion in the variety and range of objects available in Britain. Although the politician Thomas Smith complained in 1549 that England was 'overburdened with unnecessary foreign wares', imports like Venetian glass and Turkish carpets were very desirable and stimulated attempts to make copies in England. Domestic production was often achieved through the skills of European craftsmen who settled in England. From the late seventeenth century imports from Asia, Africa, the Middle East and the West Indies, such as tea, coffee, hardwoods and Indian printed cottons had an increasing impact on fashionable life. An enormous range of goods and design ideas were also exported. Textiles had been Britain's main export since the sixteenth century and the industry developed throughout the eighteenth and nineteenth centuries, harnessing new technologies, from printing techniques to steam-powered machinery. Other products of British ingenuity and skill were also exported from the end of the seventeenth century, such as precision devices (including locks) and scientific equipment, ironwares and ceramics. While handcraft techniques remained central to the production of luxury goods, many industries were transformed by the technological innovations of the eighteenth and nineteenth centuries. These developments changed the way things were made and enabled the mass production of many goods to meet the demands of the expanding population in Britain and the export markets abroad.

What Was New? New Technical Skills 1660–1710
Lock by Richard Bickford, brass, about 1669. 693-1893. **Gallery 56**

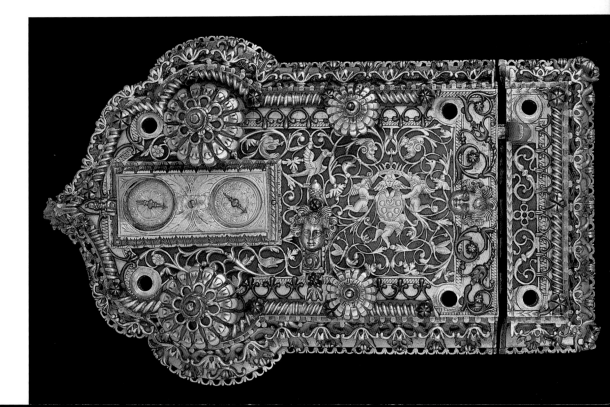

Renaissance 1500–1600

The term 'Renaissance' refers to the revival of interest in the art and culture of ancient Rome that began in Italy as early as the fourteenth century and subsequently spread throughout Europe. Renaissance style was inspired by the archaeological discovery of ancient Roman wall paintings and sculpture during the period. The shape and ornamentation of decorative objects, as well as buildings and interiors, were strongly influenced by the proportions and elements of classical architecture. The style was also characterised by an interest in naturalistic ornament. Key decorative features were masks, heads in roundels (from Roman coins), grotesques (plants and fantastic creatures copied from Roman wall paintings), strapwork (flattened bands, resembling straps of leather), moresques (flat, scrolling patterns derived from Islamic art, also known as arabesques) and bunches of fruit and flowers.

Renaissance style developed in England, Wales and Scotland throughout the sixteenth century and was regularly revived in the eighteenth and nineteenth centuries. It often combined Renaissance motifs with traditional Gothic features and heraldry to create a particularly British interpretation of the style.

This object is a 'salt' [1], used to hold the salt at dinner. It was a ceremonial showpiece placed in front of the most important dinner guest or at the head of the table. Rich patrons commissioned salts to show off their wealth, while makers displayed their mastery of technique and style. This one, the tallest surviving salt in Britain, was commissioned from a London goldsmith by a Welsh family called Mostyn and made in 1586–7. It is a good example of English Renaissance style, both in its shape, which is essentially a column, and its decoration, which is arranged in horizontal divisions. Bunches of fruit and leaves enclosed by strapwork cover the surface of the salt. This rich naturalistic ornament became increasingly popular in the later sixteenth century.

1 The Mostyn Standing Salt, silver gilt, hallmark for 1586–7. 146-1886

The Court of Henry VIII, 1509–1547

Henry VIII, keen to present himself as a powerful and cultured monarch, was a great patron of the arts. With over fifty royal residences he spent lavishly on furnishings, paintings, tapestries and silver and many of the objects made for his magnificent court reveal the influence of new ideas and designs from Renaissance Europe.

This writing box [2], made about 1525, may be a rare survival from Henry's court. It bears the arms and emblems of the king and his first queen, Katherine of Aragon, and the high quality of the decoration also suggests that it was associated with royal circles. Similar boxes were listed in court inventories and this one may have been given to a courtier or ambassador as a gift from the king.

The box is richly decorated according to Tudor taste in a combination of European Renaissance ornament and English decoration such as heraldry. It is lined with red velvet and the surfaces are covered with painted and gilded leather. The heads in roundels at the front of the box are Paris and Helen of Troy, figures from classical mythology. The inner lid shows Henry's coat of arms with the gods Mars and Venus on either side. These figures were copied from designs by the German artist Hans Burgkmair. St George, the patron saint of England, is also depicted with the dragon at his feet.

2 Writing box, wood, covered with painted and gilded leather, about 1525. W.29-1932

Skills from Europe 1500–1600

Craftsmen came to Britain from all over Europe in the sixteenth century. The skills of making inlaid furniture, arms and armour, glass and goldsmith's work were all associated with immigrant makers who settled particularly in London, East Anglia and elsewhere in the south east of England.

In 1567 Jean Carré, from Arras in France, began making Venetian glass at the Crutched Friars Glasshouse in London. Venetian glass commanded high prices because of its beauty and scarcity. Traditional English glass was made with potash and was greenish in colour; Venetian glass was made with soda and, most importantly, was clear. It was also lighter in weight and could be worked into elaborate shapes. Carré employed a Venetian glassmaker called Giacomo Verzelini, who went on to manage the glasshouse after his death. Verzelini applied for a licence from Elizabeth I for a monopoly over the manufacture of crystal drinking-glasses. This aroused hostility from native English glassmakers and merchants who protested that it would damage their trade. Nevertheless, in 1574 Verzelini obtained his monopoly, which also prohibited other merchants from importing Venetian glass.

This diamond-engraved glass dated 1581 [3] is a rare survival from Verzelini's glasshouse. Diamond engraving had been used in Roman times but was rediscovered by a Venetian in the early sixteenth century. The decoration with its stag, wave border and trees (their leaves drawn in spirals) is typical of the engraving on glasses attributed to Verzelini. It was almost certainly engraved by Anthony de Lysle, a French immigrant who was mentioned in a London parish register as 'graver in puter [pewter] and glasse'.

3 Wine glass, by Giacomo Verzelini, soda glass, dated 1581. C.523-1936

The Book 1500–1600

Johann Gutenberg's invention of printing with moveable type (separately cast metal letters) in Germany in the 1450s revolutionised European book production. William Caxton probably learnt the technique in Germany and brought it to his native England, where he opened a workshop in Westminster, London, in 1476. At first the trade remained dependent on foreign supplies of type and illustration woodblocks. Scholarly books in Latin continued to be imported, but official publications, literature and religious texts were printed in English. Books were usually sold unbound, or in simple paper or vellum covers, and the owner then had them bound. Bookbinding was a skilled craft and beautifully finished volumes were a sign of taste and status.

The Grete [Great] Herball [4], published in 1526, was the first herbal printed in England. A herbal contains information about plants and this one, translated from a French book, is illustrated with striking woodcuts. The author describes each plant with its habitat and medicinal properties. The entry for water lilies, for example, says that it is 'an herb that groweth in water… Syrups and drinks is made against hot aches and for the liver in this manner. The flowers be sodden in water and sugar put thereto and thereof is the syrup made'.

4 *The Grete Herball,* printed by Peter Treveris in 1526. L.1059-1901

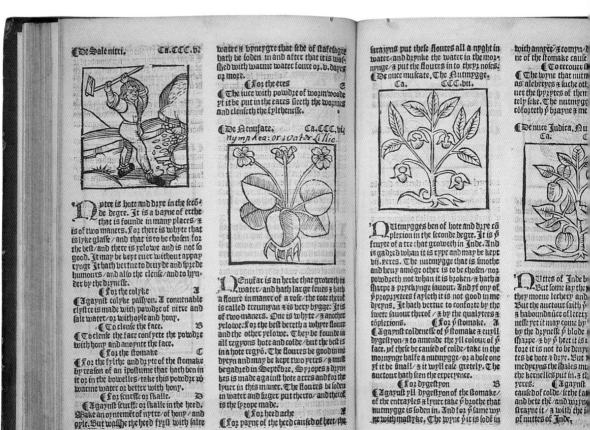

Birth, Marriage and Death 1500–1700

Birth, marriage and death were marked by rituals and ceremonies that had both social and religious significance. In a society where adults were lucky to live beyond forty-five, and around half of the children died before their tenth birthday, people were particularly conscious of death. Monuments in Church served the same purpose as *memento mori* ('remember death') imagery on jewellery, stained glass and other decorative objects – reminding people of their mortality, in the hope that they would live good Christian lives.

Sir Augustine Nicolls was a judge from Faxton in Northamptonshire who travelled 'on circuit' to try cases in different parts of the country. In 1616 he died away from home and was buried in the Lake District. His life was commemorated back in Faxton by this monument [5] which was placed on the wall of the parish church (since demolished).

The monument follows standard conventions of the time, with Sir Augustine kneeling in prayer, dressed in his red judge's robes. Traces of paint and gilding suggest it was originally bright and colourful, despite its sombre purpose. Above the figure is the Nicolls coat of arms with statues representing the virtues of Fortitude and Temperance on either side. Fortitude traditionally holds a column to represent her strength while Temperance pours water from a jug into a bowl to dilute wine. Justice and Prudence stand on either side of Nicolls. These qualities were particularly important for a judge and would have been deliberately chosen for his monument.

5 Monument to Sir Augustine Nicolls, probably by Nicholas Stone, marble and alabaster, about 1616.
A.9-1965

The Court of Elizabeth I, 1558–1603

Elizabeth I was skilful in controlling and promoting her image to create the impression of a stable monarchy. Her highly stylised portrait became familiar through prints that were widely distributed, while the queen also presented images of herself to many of her favourites. Her courtiers similarly used the arts to impress and influence others, competing to display their loyalty to the queen with costly gifts such as miniatures in lockets or jewelled cases.

This remarkable jewel [6] was given by the queen to Sir Francis Drake, possibly after the victory over the Spanish Armada in 1588. The elaborate jewelled case is set with table-cut rubies and diamonds and hung with small pearls. The front of the jewel is set with a sardonyx cameo, with the brown and white layers of the stone carved with the heads of a black man and a white woman, possibly representing the continents of Africa and Europe. At the back of the jewel, hidden beneath a lid, is a portrait of Elizabeth by the great English miniaturist Nicholas Hilliard. Inside the lid is a painting of a phoenix, one of the queen's personal emblems.

Drake had taken part in one of the earliest English voyages to West Africa in 1568 and was the first Englishman to sail around the world. Perhaps Elizabeth, who had supported many of his ventures, thought this cameo was a suitable gift for the famous navigator. Two portraits of Drake wearing the locket survive, displaying both his favour with the queen and his loyalty to her.

6 The Drake Jewel, containing a miniature by Nicholas Hilliard, dated 1588. Anonymous loan

The Great Bed of Ware

The Great Bed of Ware [7] is one of the most celebrated objects in the Museum. It was probably made for an inn at Ware, Hertfordshire, about 1590. Although it was not unusual for several guests at an inn to share a bed, this one is particularly large – at over three metres wide (ten feet) it is twice the size of a normal bed of the period. It was already a tourist attraction by 1596, when it was mentioned by a German visitor to Ware, and a few years later Sir Toby Belch in Shakespeare's *Twelfth Night* described a sheet as 'big enough for the bed of Ware'. Some of the tales surrounding the bed were exaggerated – on the night of William and Mary's coronation in 1689 it was said to have slept '26 butchers and their wives'.

The bed is similar in both form and decoration to others at the time, though it is particularly richly carved and was once brightly painted. Traces of red, green and yellow are still visible. The headboard is decorated with marquetry panels inspired by design prints from Flanders (now Belgium). They are typical of work made by German craftsmen working in Southwark in London, where there was a significant community of European immigrants.

The hangings on an Elizabethan bed were usually more expensive than the bed itself and an important sign of wealth. Heavy hangings were also practical, giving privacy and keeping out cold draughts. Here the mattresses, bed linen, wool and silk cover and woollen hangings are all modern reproductions that have been re-created using archive accounts, archaeological fragments and samples of fabric surviving from the period.

7 The Great Bed of Ware, oak with
marquetry panels, about 1590.
W.47-1931

Jacobean 1600–1625

The Jacobean period (from 'Jacobus', meaning James in Latin) is named after James VI of Scotland who succeeded Elizabeth I in 1603 to become James I of England and Wales. Jacobean style was robust and colourful. It was increasingly influenced not only by European design, but also by imports from Asia, Africa and the Americas as a result of increased international trade and exploration. In the Jacobean display are vessels made of lustrous mother-of-pearl from the Pacific Ocean and a cabinet painted in imitation of Japanese lacquer. Three-dimensional architectural effects were particularly important in Jacobean furniture, which was often deeply carved and decorated with inlay.

Isaac Oliver's miniature portrait [8] of Richard Sackville, 3rd Earl of Dorset, painted in 1616 exemplifies the exuberance and vibrancy of Jacobean style. Sackville was notoriously extravagant and dressed at the height of fashion. His stockings and doublet are heavily embroidered in silks and gold and silver thread. This delight in pattern and luxurious materials is typically Jacobean and required great skill and virtuosity from portrait painters. These details are echoed in the rich fringing on the curtains and table cover, and above all in the imported Turkish carpet. A carpet like this would have been very expensive and more likely to be placed on a table as a cover than kept on the floor.

8 Portrait miniature of Richard Sackville, 3rd Earl of Dorset, by Isaac Oliver, watercolour on vellum, dated 1616. 721-1882

Dressing for Magnificence 1600–1630

The nobility displayed their social status and wealth by dressing magnificently. For this both men and women required elaborate clothing and accessories such as shoes, lace collars, gloves, purses and jewellery.

This pair of objects [9] – the portrait and the embroidered jacket – is a unique survival from the seventeenth century. The portrait shows Margaret Laton, the wife of a Yeoman of the King's Jewel House, about 1620. She is wearing the very same jacket, with a lace edged ruff, a black gown and a lace apron; under the jacket she would have worn a linen smock. The painter has not been identified but the style is very similar to that of Marcus Gheeraerts, the most fashionable portraitist of the day.

The jacket is made of linen, finely embroidered with coloured silk flowers, birds, butterflies and insects among coiled silver-gilt leafy tendrils and shiny spangles (sequins). Naturalistic embroidery like this is typically English and the portrait shows that its colours would have originally have been more vibrant. The edges of the jacket are embellished with silver and silver-gilt bobbin lace and spangles.

Embroidered jackets, very fashionable for wealthy women at this time, would have been worn informally at home. There were several levels of formality in dress but even casual garments were made of costly materials. Very few women's clothes survive from this period because it was normal to alter clothing to follow new fashions; once garments were out of fashion they were often cut up and the pieces reused to make hangings or cushion covers. However, several of these jackets have survived, probably because they were valued for their exquisite needlework.

9 Embroidered jacket, linen, about 1610, and companion portrait attributed to Marcus Gheeraerts the younger, oil on panel, about 1620.
T.228-1994 and E.214-1994

The Court 1603–1649

10 Tapestry, Mortlake, wool, silk and metal thread, 1620–25. T.170-1978

The court of James I and his wife Anne of Denmark was a lively centre of the arts. James encouraged the establishment of a tapestry workshop at Mortlake on the River Thames to rival European production. The workshop employed skilled weavers from Flanders (now Belgium) whose tapestries were among the finest in the world and this one [**10**] was woven there around 1620–25 for James's son, Charles, when he was Prince of Wales.

It tells the story of the Roman goddess Venus and her lover, Mars. Neptune, the god of the sea, and Cupid, with a quiver full of arrows, plead with Venus's husband, Vulcan, to show mercy on the adulterous lovers (who

can be seen in the top left corner). The delicacy of flesh tones required the skills of a master weaver so the number of figures in this tapestry would have made it expensive. The weavers used silver and silver-gilt thread, which has tarnished to dark grey, to highlight the folds in the fabrics and embellish details in the border.

The tapestry probably hung at St James's Palace, London, which was Charles's main residence before he became king. Tapestries were very important in six-teenth and seventeenth century interiors, for which they provided colour and decoration on a grand scale. They could also be rolled up and carried from room to room, or even from palace to palace.

Marquetry 1650–1700

In the mid-seventeenth century furniture makers developed and refined the technique of marquetry, making patterns out of thin sheets (veneers) of different coloured woods. This was a particularly ingenious way of decorating pieces of furniture made of oak or pine, which were relatively cheap, with expensive woods such as ebony or walnut. The expansion of trade with Asia, the Caribbean, America, and Africa made many new and beautiful woods available, enabling complicated and colourful effects. Other imported materials such as ivory, tortoiseshell or mother-of-pearl were also incorporated into marquetry patterns, particularly on smaller decorative objects.

By the 1660s marquetry was the height of fashion for cabinets, tables and smaller items such as boxes and clock cases. This bracket clock made about 1695 [11] is decorated with repeating patterns of walnut, holly (stained green and red), box and purplewood on a sycamore ground. The domed top of the case features inlaid birds and scrolling patterns known as arabesques. A skilled cabinet-maker would have made the case, rather than the clockmaker, John Martin. Clocks like this became popular in the later seventeenth century because they were portable, and therefore practical as well as decorative. They were placed on tables and mantelpieces, or sometimes special brackets or shelves.

11 Bracket clock, marquetry of various woods with gilt-bronze mounts, about 1695. W.61-1926

Developments in Ceramics 1600–1710

The shape of these three mugs [12] originated in the Rhineland in Germany and became the standard for beer mugs all over Europe. However, they are made of quite different materials. The one on the left is Chinese porcelain, though its form was probably copied from a European prototype sent over by an English merchant. Chinese porcelain was rare in the west until the establishment of direct trading links in the seventeenth century. Its magical whiteness became the goal of the many European potters who tried various ways of making white ceramic.

One technique was to use a white tin glaze on buff-coloured earthenware. This is now known as delftware, after Delft, a town in The Netherlands that became a centre of manufacture. Imported German stoneware, like the patterned mug here, was another alternative. Unlike earthenware, the greyish stoneware clay could be fired at a very high temperature and glazed with salt, making it impervious to liquid. John Dwight, an English scholar and ceramic chemist, experimented widely in his attempts to make true porcelain. Though he failed to achieve his ultimate goal, he did develop almost white stoneware, using clay from Dorset that was superior to the German imports. The plain mug with a silver rim is an example of Dwight's salt-glazed stonewares that were widely admired at the time. In 1686 the Earl of Bedford bought six similar 'fine white mugs' at one shilling and sixpence each, nine times the cost of a mug made of ordinary brown stoneware.

12 Chinese porcelain mug, 1680–1715, German salt-glazed stoneware mug, about 1680, English salt-glazed stoneware mug with silver collar, dated 1682.
3749-1901, C.746-1923, 414:853-1885

Restoration 1660–1685

The restoration of the monarchy in 1660 ushered in a period of great opulence in English art and design. Charles II and many of his courtiers had spent much of their exile in France and The Netherlands and brought back with them a taste for the latest European styles. In domestic architecture a restrained classical style was developed, but flamboyant forms and profuse ornament were fashionable for interiors and decorative objects. Rooms were lined with rich tapestries, leatherwork or panelling and furnished with sumptuous upholstery and carved chairs with light, caned seats.

The design of this leather panel [13], made in The Netherlands around 1670, matches panels at Dyrham Park in south Gloucestershire. It is decorated with the dancing cherubs, birds and bulging swags of foliage, fruit and flowers that are characteristic of Restoration style. A growing interest in botany in the period led to increasingly naturalistic motifs and the panel includes tulips, roses and a pomegranate. The pattern has been embossed and decorated with a metallic finish and translucent red, green and yellow glazes. Leather panels were particularly popular for dining rooms because unlike tapestries they did not retain the smell of food.

13 Dutch leather panel, embossed, with metallic finish and coloured glazes, about 1670. W.67-1911

Britain and the Indies 1660–1720

In seventeenth century Britain 'the Indies' referred to the Americas, India and East Asia. The East India Company was established in 1600 to control the British spice trade around Indonesia and the importation of goods such as porcelain, tea and silk from China, lacquer from Japan, and cotton textiles from India. Many of these luxury products were made specifically for the export market and makers adapted their designs to suit western tastes. The new world of the West Indies produced important commodities such as dyestuffs, gold, precious stones, hardwoods, tobacco and sugar.

This porcelain jar [14] was made in China in the 1630s or 1640s for holding writing brushes. It was painted with flowers, tables and an incense burner. Later, in the 1660s, it was fitted with elaborate silver-gilt mounts probably by the Swiss-born goldsmith Wolfgang Howzer. Treasured objects and natural curiosities were often mounted in this way to emphasise their rarity and value. The demand for goods from the Indies also prompted European craftsmen to make imitations, such as delftware painted in imitation of blue and white porcelain, or cabinets painted ('japanned') in imitation of eastern lacquer. After about 1660 it became fashionable for the very wealthy to have whole rooms decorated with exotic schemes that often combined imported objects with British imitations.

14 Chinese porcelain jar, 1630–40, with European silver-gilt mounts, 1660–70. M.308-1962

The State Bed from Melville House

This magnificent bed [15] was made around 1700 for George, 1st Earl of Melville who was a senior courtier and had been Secretary of State for Scotland. The decoration of the bed was inspired by designs published by the influential French-trained designer Daniel Marot. It was probably carried out by Francis Lapiere, a Catholic immigrant from France who was one of the most important upholsterers to work in Britain.

The bed once stood in Melville House in Scotland in the Apartment of State. This was a series of splendid rooms reserved for entertaining important guests. State rooms were rarely used, but were an important expression of power and affluence and showed that the family could offer appropriately grand accommodation to high-ranking visitors. The bedroom was the last and most sumptuous room in a state apartment. It offered the greatest opportunity for extravagant display, with upholstery and window curtains to match the bed and rich tapestries hanging on the walls. The survival of the original Italian velvet hangings and Chinese silk linings and covers (adorned with the earl's monogram *GM*) on the Melville Bed is exceptionally rare.

Baroque 1685–1725

The Baroque style originated in Italy but its main sources of inspiration in England came from France and The Netherlands. Already familiar classical motifs such as acanthus leaves, scallop shells and playful cherubs (putti), combined with strapwork, were essential elements of the Baroque style but the overall effect of the decoration was often less crowded than the earlier Restoration style. The skills of decorative painting on walls and ceilings, carving, metalwork and upholstery flourished. Furniture was often elaborately carved and gilded or silvered to imitate solid gold or silver.

The Dutch prince William of Orange had married the English princess Mary in 1677. Initially they lived in The Netherlands, where Daniel Marot decorated their palace of Het Loo, but in 1689 they became joint monarchs of England, Scotland and Ireland. William and Mary expanded the palace of Hampton Court in the Baroque style, refurbishing a separate building called the Water Gallery for the queen to use as her private lodgings. Celia Fiennes, a visitor to Hampton Court in the 1690s, commented in her famous diary that 'the Queen took great delight' in the Water Gallery which 'opened into a balcony to the water and was decked with China and fine pictures of Court Ladyes'.

This blue and white delftware tile made in The Netherlands [16] probably came from the Water Gallery. Its decoration is based on a design by Daniel Marot and combines classical motifs with Baroque exuberance. The essentially symmetrical structure of the strapwork restrains the more dynamic features such as curling acanthus leaves and the figures of the drummer and trumpeter. Designs for William and Mary frequently included their initials and here the *WM* device is incorporated into the trumpeter's flag.

15 *(opposite)* The Melville Bed, oak and pine with Italian velvet and Chinese silk hangings probably by Francis Lapiere, about 1700.
W.35-1949

16 Tile, tin-glazed earthenware, The Netherlands, about 1694.
C.13-1956

Palladianism 1715–1760

From the 1720s Palladianism became the national style of classical architecture in Britain. It was based on the work of the Italian architect Andrea Palladio and the English architect Inigo Jones, who had introduced Palladio's work to England in the early seventeenth century. The new style was promoted by the amateur architect and patron Richard Boyle, 3rd Earl of Burlington, and his circle of architectural collaborators and aristocratic patrons.

Palladian architecture used a system of proportion that was based on the four classical columns (Doric, Ionic, Corinthian and composite) known as the orders of architecture. Its severe clarity on the exterior of buildings often contrasted with a more lavish and inventive approach on the interior. Nevertheless Palladian interiors and objects did also incorporate the classical principles of balance and symmetry, a fixed hierarchy of orna- mentation and a repertoire of classical motifs such as acanthus leaves and masks, as illustrated by this table [17]. It was designed around 1730 by the painter and architect William Kent for the gallery at Chiswick House, Lord Burlington's Palladian villa that became a landmark of the style. The shape of the table is based on the capital of a Corinthian column. This is the most ornate of the classical orders and its capital is charac- teristically formed of acanthus leaves. The adaptation of an architectural shape to a piece of furniture is typically Palladian.

17 Table, designed by William Kent, softwood with Siena marble top, 1727–32. W.14-1971

Rococo 1730–1760

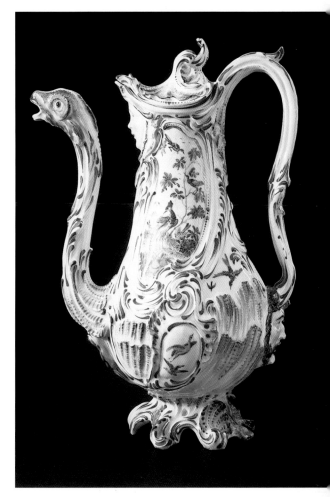

One of the paradoxes of style in the mid-eighteenth century was that severe Palladian buildings were often decorated inside in the flamboyant Rococo style. The deliberately asymmetric forms, dynamic, fluid lines and colour of the interiors were in complete contrast to the symmetry and balance of the Palladian exterior. Rococo was a style developed by makers and crafts-people rather than architects and for this reason was not used for architecture, except occasionally for garden buildings.

This coffee pot [**18**], made in Bow in London between 1760 and 1765, epitomises the Rococo style. It rests on a foot made of c-shaped scrolls that are echoed in the flowing decoration of c- and s-scrolls that cover the body of the pot. Marine motifs were particularly popular and the coffee pot is encrusted with broken shell shapes known as *rocaille;* Rococo takes its name from this French word. The marine theme is continued in the spout, which has been modelled to look like a fish head. The coffee pot has also been painted with fantastic birds that were probably inspired by designs on imported European porcelain, particularly from the Meissen factory in Germany.

18 Coffee pot, Bow, soft-paste porcelain, 1760–65. C.231-1993

Developments in the Ceramics Industry 1715–1765

Between 1715 and 1765 the manufacture of ceramics in Britain changed dramatically. During these years the Staffordshire pottery industry expanded as demand increased and this prompted potters to develop new wares, such as salt-glazed stonewares and colour-glazed earthenwares. Around 1745 British potters finally discovered a way of making porcelain and the first factories were established in London at Chelsea, Limehouse and Bow. Initially they made 'soft-paste' porcelain, which was an imitation of the true 'hard-paste' porcelains made by the Chinese, but by 1768 hard-paste porcelain was being made in Plymouth. New techniques for decorating porcelain were also developed by British makers in the period, such as transfer printing which was invented in Birmingham around 1750.

Traditionally pots and figures had been thrown on a wheel or modelled by hand. Around 1745 Staffordshire potters adopted a technique of making vessels using a plaster mould in a process known as slip-casting. The potter poured a mixture of clay and water into the plaster mould. He then allowed the water to evaporate, leaving behind a layer of clay that formed a vessel. The mould was removed and the vessel could be fired and decorated. Here is a sauceboat made in about 1760 by the slip-casting process [19] beside a block mould which was the 'master-model' used to make the individual plaster moulds. The raised, or relief decoration on this sauceboat was created by the mould and then handpainted with purple enamel. Slip-casting was an important innovation because it allowed potters to manufacture complex shapes in bulk.

19 Soft-paste porcelain sauceboat, and salt-glazed stoneware block mould, Staffordshire, 1759–60. C.665-1935, 3910-1852

Public Entertainments 1730–1760

This sculpture of the composer George Frederick Handel by Louis-François Roubiliac [20] was erected in 1738 in Spring Gardens in Vauxhall, London, on a site near the modern underground station. It is difficult now to imagine the impact it had at the time, but a public sculpture of a living person, other than a monarch or military leader, was unprecedented. Unlike most public sculpture, this figure shows Handel informally dressed and in his slippers, one of which has been discarded and lies beneath his right foot. He is holding the lyre of Orpheus, the mythological figure whose music calmed the savage beasts.

The gardens at Vauxhall were opened in the 1660s but by the 1720s had gained a reputation for debauchery and were not visited by 'polite society'. In 1728 a new proprietor, Jonathan Tyers, took over. He was an ambitious entrepreneur who aimed to combine profit with pleasure by improving the buildings and creating a venue for respectable entertainment. By 1732 he was building 'Temples, Obelisks, Triumphal Arches [and] Grotto Rooms' for which he commissioned paintings and interior decorations to create what was, effectively, the first public art gallery in Britain. Tyers also introduced orchestral music, commenting that Handel's compositions 'had so often charm'd even the greatest crowds into the profoundest calm and most decent behaviour'. Roubiliac's sculpture became so celebrated that it was used to advertise the gardens and helped to establish him as one of the leading sculptors in Britain.

20 *George Frederick Handel,* by Louis-François Roubiliac, marble, 1738. A.3-1965

Portraiture

Portraits like this [21], of couples, groups or sometimes a whole family, are known as 'conversation pieces'. They depict informal events such as a tea party or, in this example, a couple playing a duet. Music was considered to be a part of fashionable living and a sign of a good education in eighteenth century Britain. It was particularly important as a female accomplishment. Respectable men and women could enjoy performing music together even though their social life might be segregated in other ways. The artist, Arthur Devis, has followed the convention of his time by painting the woman seated, with the man standing at her side.

Devis, an artist from Lancashire, painted this unknown couple in 1749. They are well dressed but not extravagantly so, and look typical of men and women of the gentry rather than the aristocracy. Devis was popular among people who could not afford to commission the more exclusive society painters, such as Thomas Gainsborough or Joshua Reynolds. The settings in Devis's portraits did not usually represent real rooms but were idealised settings invented to illustrate the sitters' social status. Often they were copied from design books and they therefore show us what was considered a fashionable interior. Behind the couple are paintings, including landscapes, and an elegant Palladian window.

Neo-classicism 1760–1790

Neo-classicism was the leading European style of the second half of the eighteenth century. While Palladianism had been inspired by Italian classical architecture of the sixteenth century the new style, Neo-classicism, was based more directly on buildings and artefacts from ancient Rome and Greece. The Roman cities of Pompeii and Herculaneum were excavated from the late 1730s onwards and caused great excitement across Europe. Many young gentlemen, completing their education by travelling around Europe on 'the Grand Tour', saw these treasures for themselves. This rediscovery of ancient culture, painting and sculpture, as well as architecture, inspired artists and architects to create a 'true style' that could be applied in all areas of the arts. It is this universal nature of Neo-classicism that gave it such a great impact.

Key figures in the development of the style in Britain were the architects Robert Adam, William Chambers and James 'Athenian' Stuart, who had all studied in Rome. This perfume burner [22], designed by Stuart and made around 1760, was one of the earliest pieces of British Neo-classical design. It illustrates the principles of proportion and balance combined with clean lines and crisp detail that are key to the style. The burner takes the form of a tripod made up of three 'terms' (flat pillars topped with classical heads) and is decorated with classical motifs. Stuart took his inspiration from a Greek monument that he had seen in 1751.

21 (opposite) The Duet, by Arthur Devis, oil on canvas, 1749. P.31-1955

22 Perfume burner, designed by James Stuart, ormolu on marble plinth, about 1760. M.46-1948

Robert Adam and his Rivals 1770–1790

The Scottish architect Robert Adam was perhaps the single most important person in the development of Neo-classicism in eighteenth century Britain. Adam developed a highly individual and influential style and is particularly well known for designing every aspect of the interior – from decorative wall paintings and moulded ceilings to furniture and carpets. The rich colours which had been discovered in excavated Roman interiors inspired him to introduce strong colours into his own designs. Between 1773 and 1778 Robert and his brother James published their *Works in Architecture* in which they proudly claimed that they had 'introduced a great diversity' of architectural features to British interiors and 'added grace and beauty to the whole'.

This cabinet [23] was commissioned by the Duchess of Manchester to display eleven Italian *pietra dura* (hardstone) plaques showing coastal scenes. It was made around 1776 and stood in her bedchamber at Kimbolton Castle in Huntingdonshire. The cabinet is veneered in satinwood, a light coloured wood, decorated with delicate marquetry patterns in darker woods. This refined ornamentation is typical of Adam's style. On the front of the cabinet, between the plaques, are pilasters (flattened pillars) and ormolu (gilt bronze) mounts inspired by the architecture of Diocletian's palace at Spalato (now called Split, in Croatia). Adam had visited this site in 1757 and brought back drawings which he published in a lavish edition in 1764.

23 The Kimbolton Cabinet, designed by Robert Adam, various woods with *pietra dura* panels and ormolu mounts, about 1776. W.43-1949

24 *(opposite)* Furnishing fabric, printed by Robert Jones & Co., linen and cotton, 1769. T.140-1934

The Textile Printing Industry 1760–1840

The textile industry in Britain was transformed in the second half of the eighteenth century by the development of new printing techniques and processes. In the early years textiles were printed using carved wooden blocks, or in certain limited situations engraved metal plates. However, the only dye available for plate-printing was non-washable printer's ink. Francis Nixon, from Drumcondra in Ireland, was the first manufacturer to adapt the technique so that a washable dye could be used. By 1752 Nixon was advertising his 'printed Linens, done from Metal Plates (a method never before practised) with all the advantages of light and shade, in the strongest most lasting colours'. By 1757 he had brought the technique to England where it was quickly adopted by other textile printers.

This textile [24] was printed by Robert Jones, a leading English manufacturer, in 1769. Its crisp lines, seen in the tiny leaves and the texture of the stone, could only be achieved using finely engraved copper plates. In the 1780s textile printing technology developed further with the introduction of engraved metal rollers. This process was quicker and more economical than previous techniques and by the early nineteenth century it was being used for both furnishing and dress fabrics. As the industry expanded in the late eighteenth century, Lancashire took over from London as the main centre of production.

Thomas Chippendale, Entrepreneur

Thomas Chippendale is the best known British furniture designer of the eighteenth century. He came from a Yorkshire family of joiners and cabinet-makers and in his twenties moved to London where he opened a workshop in St Martin's Lane in 1753. The following year he published *The Gentleman and Cabinet-maker's Director*, a book of furniture designs that became highly influential. This page from the *Director* [25] shows the Rococo style of furniture for which Chippendale is perhaps most famous. Other designs in the book include Gothic and Chinoiserie elements, which were often combined with Rococo style in the 1750s and 1760s.

At this time cabinet-makers were taking over from upholsterers in controlling the furnishing of houses. Chippendale not only designed and made furniture but was sometimes commissioned to decorate entire rooms, including wallpaper, carpets and architectural features such as chimney-pieces.

The *Director* was so popular that a second edition was quickly published in 1755 and a revised edition in 1762. This later edition contained Neo-classical designs, showing the growing influence of the new classicism. The *Director* was also sold in North America and Europe, ensuring that Chippendale's influence was international, and the designs have continued to be reprinted to this day.

25 Plate 83 from the *Director,*
by Thomas Chippendale, 1754.
L.4674-1978

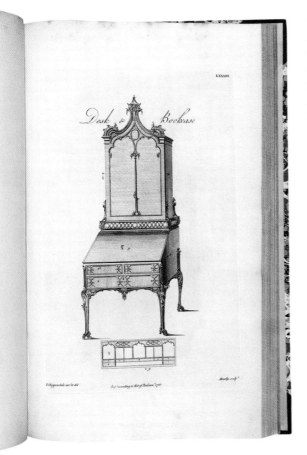

Mr and Mrs Garrick, A Fashionable Couple

David Garrick and his wife, the Austrian dancer Eva Maria Veigel, were among the most celebrated couples in eighteenth century London. They married in 1749 when Garrick was manager of the Drury Lane Theatre and at the height of his fame as an actor.

In 1754 they bought a house outside London at Hampton which they transformed into a fashionable country retreat. The Neo-classical architect Robert Adam later made improvements to the house and Lancelot 'Capability' Brown designed the gardens. The writer Samuel Johnson declared that David Garrick lived 'rather as a prince than an actor ... his table, his equipage, and manner of living, are all most expensive and equal to those of a nobleman.' Mary Delaney, a visitor to Hampton in 1770, commented that the house and its furnishings 'owe its prettiness and elegance to her [Eva Garrick's] good taste'.

The objects in the display relating to the Garricks show how the couple indulged their enthusiasm for Chinoiserie in the interiors at Hampton. Mrs Garrick's dress from the early 1760s [26] was made of yellow silk woven and painted in China. The bright greens, reds and blues of the flowers and leaves and the triple ruffled sleeves, embellished with lace, exemplify the colourful Rococo fashions of the time. A dress like this would have been worn over hoops at the hips to give the skirt the slightly square shape that was the height of fashion.

26 Mrs Garrick's robe and petticoat, painted Chinese silk, 1760–65. T.593-1999

Developments in the Metal Trades 1740 –1840

New techniques and materials in the metal trades enabled the production of increasing numbers of small decorative goods. These two little boxes [27] were made in the Midlands in 1765–75, either in Birmingham or Staffordshire. Birmingham developed such a reputation for making novelty objects that it was dubbed 'the toyshop of Europe'. These objects were not toys for children, for in the eighteenth century 'toy' simply meant a trinket or small box. The square box would have held snuff while the coiled snake box was probably for small sweets.

They are both made of copper, enamelled in bright colours. Copper had traditionally been made into sheets by laboriously hammering the metal, but now the growing use of steel rollers accelerated production. The best enamel had previously been imported, but in the mid-eighteenth century good quality enamels in fine colours were increasingly being produced in Britain. These improvements in manufacturing techniques made novelty boxes cheaper to produce and therefore available to a wider, less-wealthy market.

Greater middle-class prosperity encouraged demand for these items and snuff boxes especially were made in great numbers because of the popularity of snuff-taking. Gentility was judged, to some extent, by owning the right items and using them correctly. An elegant snuff box was an essential accessory for a fashionable gentleman.

27 Enamel boxes, 1765–75.
C.470-1914 and C.478-1914

Josiah Wedgwood, Entrepreneur

The Staffordshire potter Josiah Wedgwood was one of a new kind of entrepreneur that dominated the market after 1750. Wedgwood was unique in the pottery industry in combining a thorough knowledge of his craft with a passion for experimentation and a talent for marketing. His first big commercial success was a range of cream coloured earthenware which he named 'Queen's Ware' following an order for a tea service from Queen Charlotte in 1765. This useful marketing device ensured that Queen's Ware was a success and the profits enabled Wedgwood to fund his more experimental ceramics. Among these was the blue or green pottery with white decoration known as jasperware (a fine unglazed stoneware), which is now most closely associated with his name.

In 1768 Wedgwood formed a partnership with his friend Thomas Bentley, a Liverpool merchant who introduced him to a circle of architects and collectors; among this group was the subject of this finely modelled jasper portrait medallion [28], William Hamilton, the British ambassador to Naples. He is perhaps better known now for being the husband of Emma Hamilton, Lord Nelson's mistress.

Hamilton's collection of ancient Greek and Roman vases was an important inspiration for Wedgwood's Neo-classical work. In 1769 Wedgwood declared to Bentley that he intended to become 'vase maker General to the Universe' and he later commented that he had 'endeavoured to preserve … the elegant simplicity of the antique [or classical] forms'. Wedgwood was one of the first British potters to see his ceramics as works of art, opening exclusive showrooms and holding exhibitions of his most celebrated productions.

28 Portrait medallion of Sir William Hamilton, by Wedgwood, jasperware, first issued in 1773, this example 1780–1800. 1489-1855

Being British

29 *Salisbury Cathedral,* by John Constable, oil on canvas, 1823. FA.33

The nation of Great Britain did not exist until the Act of Union of 1707 brought Scotland under a single parliament with England and Wales. During the eighteenth century an emerging sense of national unity was strengthened by wars and constant rivalry with France over trade and empire. The display shows how, by 1810, national sentiment was often focused on naval and military heroes such as Nelson and Wellington. At the same time there was a growing romantic appreciation of Britain's history, landscape and ancient buildings, and tourists increasingly visited picturesque sites around the country. For the first time some artists, including John Sell Cotman, J. M. W. Turner and John Constable, chose landscapes as their chief subject rather than historical themes.

Constable's *Salisbury Cathedral* [**29**], painted in 1823, is a quintessentially British landscape painting with its medieval cathedral surrounded by trees, clouds and cattle drinking at the edge of a water meadow. Despite their apparent simplicity and directness, Constable's paintings were carefully chosen images of rural life created for urban viewers. He described this one as 'the most difficult subject in landscape I ever had on my easel'. It was commissioned by John Fisher, Bishop of Salisbury, who can be seen with his wife in the left-hand corner of the painting.

Thomas Hope

Classicism continued to dominate British art and design into the nineteenth century, evolving into a heavier, bolder style known as Regency Classicism. A key figure in the style was Thomas Hope, the wealthy connoisseur and collector who designed this impressive vase [30]. He based it on an ancient Greek white marble vase that he had seen in Italy in 1802, though this vase is in fact copper, treated to resemble bronze. It is decorated with applied ormolu (gilt bronze) mounts of the highest quality. Some of the gilding has a matt surface which contrasts effectively with areas of burnished, shiny gilding to highlight the decorative features of the mounts.

The vase was made in 1802–3 for Hope's London mansion in Duchess Street, which he opened to invited members of the public in 1804. His aim was to educate patrons, designers and craftsmen in the use of ornament in interior decoration and to show off his vast collection of vases, sculpture and paintings. Regency interiors were boldly coloured and richly decorated, often with a mixture of styles, and each of the rooms in Hope's house was designed in a different manner – Greek, Roman, Egyptian, Persian and Indian. In 1807 he published prints of the interiors in his *Household Furniture and Interior Decoration*, introducing the phrase 'interior decoration' to the English language. Many Regency designers adapted his ideas, though his taste was often too extravagant to be copied directly.

30 Vase, designed by Thomas Hope, copper with ormolu mounts, 1802–3. M.33-1983

Regency Classicism 1800–1830

Regency Classicism was the last stage of the Neo-classical movement that had started in the late 1750s. Although the Regency itself only lasted from 1811 to 1820, when George III was ill and his son ruled in his place, the heavier forms of Regency Classicism emerged in the early years of the century and lasted until the 1830s. One of the most innovative aspects of Regency Classicism was its combination of Greek and Roman design with contrasting elements taken from nature, the arts of ancient Egypt, the Rococo style of the mid-eighteenth century and the Empire style of Napoleonic France.

The bill for this upholstered chair [31] describes it as a *bergère,* the French word for an upholstered armchair. It was supplied in 1823 by the firm Morel & Hughes for Northumberland House in London (now demolished). The shape is based on an antique Greek form, and although bold and chunky, it retains the simple lines that are a key element of classicism. It is decorated with classical motifs such as the 'egg and dart' pattern at the top of the legs, small rosettes and curling gilded acanthus leaves around the base of the seat. Imported woods such as mahogany, rosewood and, in this case, zebrawood, were favoured for Regency furniture and the gilded carving looks particularly striking on this dark background.

31 Chair, known as a *bergère,* by Morel & Hughes, zebrawood with modern upholstery, 1823. W.48-1979

William Beckford, the Collector

32 The Beckford Cup, Indian agate
with silver-gilt mounts, hallmark for
1815–16, by James Aldridge.
428-1882

William Beckford was a collector whose enthusiasm for historical styles such as Gothic or Renaissance anticipated the revivals that became so fashionable from the 1830s. He inherited a vast fortune amassed from his family's sugar plantations, worked by slaves in Jamaica. Leaving Britain in 1784 after a sexual scandal, he spent much of the remainder of his life abroad.

Beckford was fascinated by Islamic and East Asian art and culture and had a particularly important collection of Japanese lacquer. He collected widely on his European travels and bought objects from French aristocratic collections dispersed after the Revolution of 1789. He is perhaps best known for Fonthill Abbey, his Gothic fantasy house in Wiltshire which was begun by the architect James Wyatt in 1796 and formed an ideal setting for Beckford's collection.

Beckford also commissioned new objects influenced by historical styles and, with his companion Gregorio Franchi, was actively involved in the design of many pieces. This cup [32] was intended to imitate the objects that had been part of the 'cabinets of curiosity' in the sixteenth and seventeenth centuries, when aristocratic collectors mounted valuable artefacts and natural curiosities in precious metals to emphasise their rarity. It is made of agate, a semi-precious stone, and was probably carved in northern India in the early 1800s. The London silversmith James Aldridge made the silver-gilt mounts in 1815, decorating them with Renaissance arabesque ornament based on Islamic decoration.

Gothic Revival 1830 –1880

Gothic Revival is probably the most familiar Victorian architectural style. Its coloured brick buildings with pointed arches and patterned tiles on walls and floors were based on forms and decoration used in the Middle Ages, but it also often incorporated more fanciful elements taken from romantic notions of medieval chivalry.

Although it had been used by some enthusiasts from about 1740, Gothic Revival style only began to dominate British design in the 1830s. It was applied not only to architecture, such as the Houses of Parliament that were begun in the 1840s, but also to all sorts of decorative objects and interior schemes. Gothic Revival furniture tended to be simple in shape and construction but highly decorated, like this cabinet [33] designed in 1858 by William Burges, one of the most original and inventive figures of the movement. The design was inspired by furniture dating from around 1300 that Burges had seen in cathedrals in France. Though intended to be used as a writing desk, the cabinet is architectural in form, resembling a building with a steeply pitched roof and tall pinnacles. It was decorated with scenes taken from classical and medieval history representing literature, the alphabet and printing, painted by Edward Poynter who also designed the Poynter Room in the V&A.

33 Cabinet, designed by William Burges and painted by Edward Poynter, pine and mahogany with iron locks and hinges, about 1858. Circ. 217-1961

The Church 1840 –1900

There was a powerful religious revival in Britain in the nineteenth century as various Christian denominations took up the challenge of building new churches and chapels for the growing population. The government set aside money for the construction of new churches and many neglected Anglican churches were restored and refurbished, often in the Gothic style. Roman Catholics, who were allowed to worship freely for the first time since the Protestant Reformation, began to build their own highly decorated churches. Also, some within the Church of England were keen to revive pre-Reformation forms of worship and church decoration, while Methodists and other non-conformists favoured undecorated chapels and were opposed to elaborate ritual.

This cope and hood [34], worn by the priest during Catholic services, were designed by A. W. N. Pugin, an architect who was one of the most passionate proponents of the Gothic style. He was a prolific designer of religious objects and conceived them for the Catholic church of St Augustine, which he built in the grounds of his home in Ramsgate, Kent in the 1840s. The hood is embroidered with the head of St Thomas. The pattern of the fabric used for the cope is called 'Gothic Tapestry' and was based on Italian velvets of the fourteenth and fifteenth century. Pugin wrote 'I am delighted with the stuff'. The fabric was not only used for religious vestments but also for secular interior decoration schemes in the Gothic style.

34 Cope and hood, designed by A. W. N. Pugin, silk and wool, 1848–50. T.289- and 287-1989

The Great Exhibition 1851

35 Vases, by Charles Meigh & Son,
stoneware, about 1851.
Circ. 481- and 374-1963

The Great Exhibition of Works of Industry of All Nations, held in London in 1851, was the first international fair. It was designed to show manufacturing goods and new technology from all over the world and to promote international trade. The exhibition took place in Hyde Park in a revolutionary pre-fabricated building of glass and iron covering nineteen acres, nicknamed the 'Crystal Palace'.

These vases [35] were made by the Staffordshire firm of Charles Meigh & Son and won a prize medal at the exhibition. As exhibition pieces they were designed to advertise the firm's technical brilliance. They are decorated with images of the Crystal Palace and Queen Victoria and her husband, Prince Albert, who was an instrumental figure behind the exhibition. The queen later recalled the opening ceremony: 'The tremendous cheering, the joy expressed in every face, the vastness of

the building … and my beloved Husband the creator of this great "Peace Festival", uniting the industry and art of all nations of the earth, all this, was indeed moving'. She described it as 'the happiest, proudest day of my life', and visited thirty-four times.

The Great Exhibition captured the popular imagination, attracting more than six million visitors from all over the country, many travelling on the new steam trains for the first time. Its success dispelled the myth that working class people were not interested in culture. Profits from the exhibition secured a site for the South Kensington Museum, which later became the Victoria and Albert Museum, and a selection of 244 objects was bought from the exhibition to form part of the museum's first collections. The Crystal Palace was later moved to south London where it remained until destroyed by fire in 1936.

Technological Innovations 1850–1900

The Victorians witnessed a remarkable transformation of their world as new technologies affected every area of industrial production and domestic life. The display on technological innovations shows the wide range of goods that became available, such as decorative metalwares, papier mâché, pressed glass and textiles made on the revolutionary jacquard loom. Industrialisation, which had brought cheaper goods to the middle classes in the eighteenth century, now made them affordable to virtually all levels of society and images of Victorian sitting rooms often show them full of furniture and ornaments.

One of the most startling changes was in colour. In 1856 a young chemist, William Perkin, created a black sludge in the course of an experiment. Perkin was naturally curious and began to examine it, discovering that in certain circumstances it turned a clear, brilliant purple. He had accidentally created a synthetic dye, known as mauveine, or aniline purple.

Until this discovery dyes were derived from plants or insects and were complicated to produce. Perkin's discovery created an entirely new industry and sparked off frantic research across Europe that resulted in a whole range of new chemical dyes derived from coal tar and other substances. The benefits of synthetic dyes that were much less laborious to produce and created vivid new colours caused a sensation. The range of colours that became available can be seen in this book of commercial dye samples of 1896 [36] from the German company Bayer, including 'Alkali Blue', 'Bismark Brown' and 'Acid Magenta'. The new colours were soon used in the manufacture of both furnishings and dress and the new technology made them widely available across the social spectrum.

36 Dye sample book, F. Bayer & Co.,
wool and silk samples on paper,
1896. T.173-1985

Technological Innovations: Photography

In 1835 William Henry Fox Talbot invented the photographic negative. Talbot's invention created photography as we know it for it enabled an unlimited number of positive prints, or photographs, to be taken from a negative. Talbot called his process 'calotype', from the Greek word *kalos* meaning beautiful. Another technique developed in France at around the same time was called the daguerreotype after its inventor Louis Daguerre. It created images of beautiful clarity but they could not be reproduced because each image was unique, produced directly onto a silvered copper plate without a negative.

The daguerreotype continued to be used by professional photographers, especially for portraits, because the images were of good quality. However, from the early 1850s it was overtaken by more commercial processes, used by professionals and amateurs alike, which involved printing from glass negatives onto paper. An extraordinary number of photographic techniques and printing processes were invented, often by amateurs, and all sorts of surprising materials were used including albumen (from egg white), gelatine, salt, iron, silver and platinum.

The first photographic techniques required subjects to pose for several minutes, which is partly why they often look so stiff and serious. As photography developed the exposure time was reduced and photographs could be more spontaneous. This photograph was taken in 1898 [**37**] and is an example of an early 'snapshot'. It captures a light-hearted moment and celebrates the new pastime of cycling. In the 1880s small light cameras, fast film and factory processing of negatives encouraged enthusiastic and inventive amateur photographers.

French Style 1830–1880

French style was the most commercially successful style for interior decoration in Britain and Europe in the nineteenth century. Characterised by strong colours, rich textures and gilding, it included revivals of styles that had been fashionable in France between 1660 and 1790. They were often identified by the name of the French king at the time when they were first popular – Louis XIV, Louis XV or Louis XVI.

This gilt brass inkstand [**38**], made about 1880, epitomises the Louis XV style. Its curling, c-shaped scrolls and ornate rock and shell forms (*rocaille*) are reminiscent of the Rococo style that had been so popular during his reign in the mid-eighteenth century. The inkstand contains brass ink pots with lids decorated with *rocaille* and stylised flowers while a figure of Cupid is striding over a rock to present a letter.

French style was at first used by royalty and the aristocracy and was associated with luxury and glamour. Improvements in manufacturing techniques then reduced production costs and meant that manufacturers could adapt the style for a wide range of markets. Although widely popular in nineteenth century Britain, French style was not universally admired. Some designers thought it was too fussy and criticised it as unimaginative because it revived historical styles from the past rather than creating new ones.

37 *(opposite)* Photograph from an album, platinum print, 1898.
E.2283-1997

38 Inkstand, gilt brass, about 1880.
M.3-1994

Antique Collecting

Collecting had once been the preserve of the very wealthy and involved mostly Greek and Roman antiquities and Old Master paintings. In the Victorian period it became a more popular interest and a much wider range of antiques was acquired, often specifically to furnish interiors. This growth of interest led to the rise of the antique shop, the specialist society and the professional dealer.

These objects [39] once belonged to the rich collectors Lady Charlotte Schreiber and her husband Charles. They were passionate about antiques, collecting fans, enamels and playing cards as well as ceramics. The Schreibers became acknowledged experts on English ceramics within a wide circle of dealers, museum curators and amateur collectors. In 1884, after her husband's death, Lady Schreiber donated the collection to the South Kensington Museum (later the V&A).

The oldest object in the group is the tin-glazed earthenware container in the shape of a cat, dated 1676. When she first saw it Lady Schreiber described it as 'hideous'; nevertheless she bought it because she knew it was rare and an important addition to the collection. She was similarly attracted to the salt-glazed teapot made in Staffordshire around 1740, which she thought 'very ugly' but 'very desirable'. The Staffordshire sauce-boat made around 1760 was bought from a Bristol china dealer in 1869. In December 1879 Schreiber visited a new dealer in Oxford Street where she saw the porcelain lidded vase, made in Bristol around 1775, priced at £150. Four days later she returned with her husband and successfully bargained with the dealer, eventually paying £75.

Celebration and Commemoration 1837 –1901

Queen Victoria reigned for sixty-four years and became a national and imperial icon. The events of her life were the subject of constant public interest and were celebrated in sculpture, songsheets, paintings and commemorative pottery. This royal souvenir industry was not new in the nineteenth century, but it expanded during Victoria's reign and became hugely profitable.

The cult of personality was not just focused on Victoria, but also on her husband, Prince Albert, who died in 1861. In January 1862 a committee was formed to help the grieving queen decide on a monument to commemorate his life. The architect George Gilbert Scott was chosen as the designer and this model [40] was made so that Victoria could see his proposal in three dimensions.

The magnificent Albert Memorial was erected between 1863 and 1876 in Kensington Gardens, where it can still be seen. The decoration reflects the interests of the prince. It shows him surrounded by statues representing Agriculture, Commerce, Manufactures and Engineering and the four continents, Africa, Asia, Europe and America. The reliefs below the statues contain portraits of sculptors, musicians, poets and painters. It cost £120,000, much of it raised by public subscription, reflecting the initial sympathy for the queen who was devastated by Albert's death.

The model differs slightly from the final sculpture in Kensington Gardens. Albert holds a scroll in his hand in the model, while on the finished monument he holds a copy of the 1851 Great Exhibition catalogue in recognition of his guiding role in that venture.

39 (Opposite) Ceramics from the Schreiber Collection, bought between 1869 and 1884.
414:821-1885, 414:740-1885,
414:891-1885, 414:984-1885

40 Model for the Albert Memorial, designed by Sir George Gilbert Scott, plaster, 1863. A.13-1973

Protecting New Designs

The growing market for decorative goods in the nine-teenth century stimulated thousands of new designs for the shape and ornamentation of objects. Firms, designers and makers in competition with each other feared that their work could be copied by a rival designer or factory and some commentators were concerned that this might have a damaging effect on British business. In 1842 new laws were introduced to combat the problem. There were two forms of legal protection: *patents,* which were granted to protect inventions, and *design registration,* which was used for protecting designs such as an ornamental pattern or the shape of a teapot. Objects with a registered design were marked with a unique number or diamond mark that indicated the date of registration. This was also a useful marketing device since the registration mark acted as a mark of authenticity and helped guard against fakes and imitations.

Registration was enforced by the courts and a firm that illegally used a registered design could be sued. The biscuit makers, Huntley & Palmers, made the mistake of not registering the design of either the image or the shape of this biscuit tin of 1894 [**41**]. Two years later another firm, Burgess & Leigh, registered the identical shape and pattern for a teapot and Huntley & Palmers threatened to sue. However, the two firms reached a compromise and the case never came to court. It was agreed that Burgess & Leigh could continue to use the shape, but the teapot was to be decorated with only one colour, rather than the original multi-coloured design that is shown here.

41 Earthenware teapot by Burgess & Leigh, 1896, and biscuit tin by Huntley & Palmers, 1894.
C.277-1983 and M.257-1983

The Freelance Designer: Christopher Dresser

42 Soup tureen and ladle, designed by Christopher Dresser, electroplate with ebony handles, 1880. M.26-1972

Christopher Dresser was one of the most innovative designers of the nineteenth century. He ran his own studio in London, marketing his designs to some of the leading firms and manufacturers in Britain. His prolific output included furniture and furnishing fabrics, ceramics, glass and electroplated tableware. Dresser believed passionately that design should be functional and that 'utility and beauty must be characteristic of every object'. He also recognised that good design could be affordable to a wide public if cheaper materials and methods of manufacture were used. He is sometimes called the first industrial designer because, unlike some of his contemporaries, he enthusiastically embraced new technologies and designed for industrial manufacture.

Dresser began his career in 1854 as a lecturer in the application of botany to design and his work was often characterised by organic, natural shapes and motifs. Like many other designers of his time, he studied art and artefacts from other cultures and he particularly admired Persian and South American traditions. In 1877 he visited Japan and his appreciation of Japanese art and design had a great impact on his work. The simplicity of this striking tureen and ladle [**42**], made in 1880, reflects his admiration for Japanese design, while the handles are influenced by Japanese bamboo handles though they are made of ebonised wood. Dresser was particular about the placing of feet, handles and spouts on objects to make them more functional and the three feet give this tureen stability. He also replaced the traditional curved handle of the ladle with a more angular shape that needs only the slightest turn for serving.

Influences from beyond Europe 1840–1900: India

Although British travellers and merchants had travelled beyond Europe for many centuries, trade and empire expanded dramatically in the nineteenth century. India, as a key colony, had a significant effect on British style.

Indian motifs were incorporated into British textiles but often with European rather than Indian colours, resulting in designs that would have seemed as exotic to an Indian as to a British person. A good example of this is the woven paisley shawl [43]. From the early 1800s Europeans were importing woven shawls from Kashmir in northern India decorated with a traditional leaf motif called a *buta*. By the 1850s the industry was increasingly geared towards the export market and French and British agents brought pattern books for Indian weavers to copy. The *buta* motif became elongated and covered more of the surface of the shawl than on a traditional Kashmiri design.

Paisley in Scotland was one of the first British centres to make imitations of these shawls and the adoption of the jacquard loom in the 1840s enabled them to produce goods that were cheaper than Indian imports. The pattern (now known as 'paisley') became even more stylised and further removed from the Indian original. The naturalistic motifs on the Scottish shawl and the burgundy colour are distinctly European elements, while the elongated pine cone and *buta* forms are derived from Indian motifs.

43 Detail from an Indian pashmina shawl *(above)* and Scottish wool shawl *(left)*, about 1850–55.
772-1852 and T.111-1977

Advertising Posters

By 1875 advances in printing by lithography enabled the mass-production of large-scale colour posters for the first time. In the growing consumer market of the late nineteenth century they were used with great effect to advertise products and services. 'Posted' on street hoardings they transformed towns and cities, while smaller posters could be shown on the side of trams and buses, in shop windows and behind the counter. Artists welcomed the new medium as an exciting and liberating means of expression. Inspired by French pioneers, British designers like Dudley Hardy, John Hassall and the partnership known as The Beggarstaffs used their talents in this new form of public art.

Posters and packaging were used to develop distinctive and recognisable brand images for products and companies, sometimes with humorous characters and catch phrases. This poster [44] was designed around 1899 by Hassall who believed that a successful advertisement 'should hit the passer-by right in the eyeball'. It refers to the 'gold rush' of the 1890s, when thousands of men ventured to the Klondyke valley in Canada in the hope of finding their fortune. The gold rush captured the imagination of people in Britain as well as America and Canada and this poster shows a returning prospector reviving himself with a hot foot bath of Colman's mustard.

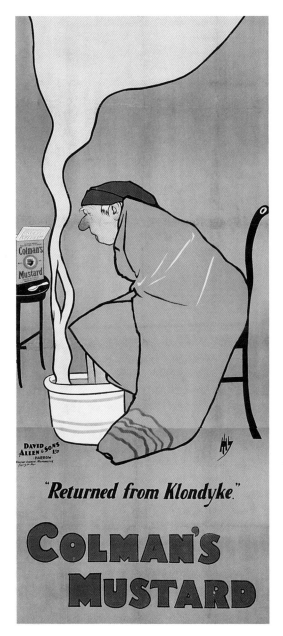

44 Poster for Colman's mustard, designed by John Hassall, colour lithograph, about 1899. E.23-1973

Birth, Marriage and Death 1850–1900

45 Wedding dress, silk-satin with Honiton appliqué lace, machine net and bobbin lace, 1865. T.43-1947

There were rigid codes of behaviour relating to birth, marriage and death in the Victorian period, with special outfits and gifts that reflected social status. The behaviour of the queen had a significant influence on these customs and people were expected to 'go into mourning' not just after the death of a member of their own family, but also after that of a member of the Royal Family.

This wedding dress [45] was worn by Eliza Penelope Clay for her marriage to Joseph Bright in London in 1865 and is similar to that worn by Queen Victoria for her marriage in 1840. Victoria had broken royal tradition by wearing a relatively simple gown, unlike the heavily ornate dresses of some of her predecessors. The plain ivory silk of Eliza Clay's dress was trimmed with Honiton lace from Devon, which had also been used on Victoria's dress. The gown has a fashionably wide skirt supported by a crinoline – a cage made of steel hoops worn under the skirt and petticoats. Brides had not always worn white but by 1800 it had become more common than any other colour, at least among the wealthy. White was considered appropriate for young brides because it symbolised purity. Less well off, or older, brides tended to wear a coloured dress that could be worn again on other special occasions. Some brides began to wear veils around 1800, though they also wore bonnets decorated with ribbons and flowers.

Eating and Drinking 1870–1900

Entertaining at home became popular among the Victorian middle classes and a great diversity of objects was increasingly available for the fashionable hostess, from tablewares to centrepieces for displaying flowers and sweets. By the 1860s a new way of serving dinner had transformed the look of the dining table. Previously dishes were set out on the table for diners to help themselves; now each course was served *à la Russe,* directly to the guests by servants, and the place setting (or 'cover') became more important as cutlery and plates for each course were laid out.

This place setting [46] is based on an illustration in the 1888 edition of Mrs Beeton's famous book, *Household Management.* This was the most popular and authoritative of a growing number of books that not only provided recipes but also described how to set and decorate the table and gave advice on how to select a menu, serve the food and entertain the guests. Here the cutlery is set out for four courses (soup, fish, and two meat courses) with glasses for wine, champagne and sherry. Mrs Beeton advised that champagne could be drunk 'with the joints' of meat. Sherry was taken with the early courses and sometimes at the end with dessert. The two enamelled silver salt cellars are both decorative and practical; Mrs Beeton stated that 'there should be a salt cellar between every two persons'.

With fewer dishes on the table there was space for elaborate decorations. Here a glass comport, or stand, holds colourful fruit and a pressed glass bowl in the shape of a swan is full of flowers. Hostesses competed with each other to create lavish displays and often they spent more on flowers, plants, decorative fruit and even trees than on the food itself.

46 Place setting, 1864–1904.
M.30-2000, M.33 to 39-2000, Circ.748-1967,
M.29-1983, C.270-1987, C.37-2000,
C.40-2000, C.36-2000

William Morris

William Morris was one of the most significant figures
in Victorian art and design. He was a poet, writer,
conservationist and active socialist, as well as an
inspired designer whose wallpaper and textile patterns
are still familiar today. In 1860 Morris set about redecor-
ating his home, the Red House in Bexleyheath, Kent,
which had been designed by his friend, the architect
Philip Webb. This experience persuaded Morris to set
up a company with friends. Morris, Marshall, Faulkner
& Co. was established in 1861 and became Morris &
Co. in 1875. Both firms produced and sold furniture,
textiles, wallpaper and stained glass designed by Morris
and other artists and designers. In 1877 Morris & Co.
opened a shop in Oxford Street in London, supplying a
wide range of furnishings for the home.

The firm also decorated whole interiors for private
clients. This carpet [47], designed and woven in
collaboration with his assistant, J.H. Dearle, was made
in 1889 for the drawing room at Bullerswood in
Chislehurst, Kent, a house belonging to a wool trader
called John Sanderson. Morris's fascination with
colour, pattern and texture found its perfect expression
in the design of carpets. He was particularly inspired
by antique Turkish and Persian carpets, which he
collected, and some important examples in the V&A
were bought on his advice.

47 The Bullerswood Carpet,
designed by William Morris and
J.H.Dearle, wool, 1889. T.31-1923

Arts and Crafts 1860–1910

The Arts and Crafts movement produced one of the most original styles of the nineteenth century. The men and women of the movement were dismayed by the social effects of industrialisation, which intensified in the nineteenth century, and instead encouraged the revival of traditional handcraft techniques and working methods. William Morris and Charles Robert Ashbee were two of the key figures in the movement. Ashbee formed the Guild of Handicraft in London in 1888 but later moved to Chipping Campden in Gloucestershire. The Guild, which produced beautifully designed furniture, silver, enamels, leather and metalwork, was a community of makers, some with no previous training who learnt their skills by trial and error.

An important principle of the Arts and Crafts movement was that decoration should reflect the method of making. On this decanter [48], designed by Ashbee around 1904, the construction of the silver mounts is visible. The hammer marks show that the mounts have been handmade, and the points at which the silver wires have been soldered are not hidden but made a decorative feature. The linear elegance and simplicity of this decanter are typical of Ashbee's later style. Its shape is based on a seventeenth century wine bottle found during the building of his house in Chelsea. Decoration is concentrated on the finial, a discreet feature on the lid, incorporating a semi-precious stone called a chrysoprase.

48 Decanter, designed by C.R. Ashbee, glass with silver mounts, hallmark for 1904–5. M.121-1966

Reigns of the Tudor monarchs of England	Reigns of the Stuart monarchs of Scotland	Entries highlighted in blue followed by bracketed numbers relate to objects illustrated in this guide book
		Political and cultural events in Britain and the world
1485–1509 **Henry VII**	**1488–1513** **James IV**	**1492** Columbus sails to America
		1497 Vasco da Gama sails to India; John Cabot lands in Newfoundland
		1500
1509-1547 **Henry VIII** [2]	**1513–1542** **James V**	**1515–30** Building of Hampton Court Palace
		1516 First European ship (Portuguese) reaches China
		1517 Beginning of the Reformation in Germany
		1519–22 Ferdinand Magellan's ships sail around the world
		1525
		1526 Babur captures Delhi and founds the Mughal Empire
		1532 The painter Hans Holbein the younger settles in England
		1533 Henry VIII divorces Katherine of Aragon and marries Anne Boleyn
		1534 Act of Supremacy makes Henry VIII head of the Church of England
		1535 Miles Coverdale publishes the first complete Bible in English
		1536 Union of England and Wales
		1536–9 Dissolution of the Monasteries
1547–1553 **Edward VI**	**1542–1567** **Mary Queen of Scots**	**1541** Henry VIII proclaims himself King of Ireland
		1550
1553–1558 **Mary I**		**1553** Lady Jane Grey is Queen of England for 9 days
		1556 Akbar becomes Mughal Emperor
		1562 John Hawkins's first expedition to West Africa where he buys slaves
1558–1603 **Elizabeth I** [6]	**1567–1625** **James VI**	**1567** New Testament translated into Welsh; Venetian glass is first made in England [3]
		1568 Mary Queen of Scots flees to England
		1570 Andrea Palladio's *Four Books of Architecture* published in Italy [17]
		1575
		1577–80 Francis Drake's circumnavigation of the world
		1584 Walter Raleigh establishes an English colony in Virginia, America
		1587 Mary Queen of Scots is beheaded
		1588 English defeat the Spanish Armada [6]
		1596 Great Bed of Ware is recorded by a German tourist [7]
		1598 Edict of Nantes grants toleration to Protestants in France
		1599 Globe Theatre is built on the banks of the River Thames
		1600
Reigns of the Stuart monarchs of England, Scotland and Ireland		**1600** English East India Company is founded
		1602 Dutch East India Company is founded
		1604 Isaac Oliver becomes miniature painter to Anne, Queen of James I [8]
1603–1625 James I Union of the Crowns of England and Scotland: James VI of Scotland becomes James I of England, Wales and Ireland [8]		**1605** Gunpowder Plot fails and Guy Fawkes executed
		1609 East India Company establishes a trading post at Hirado, Japan
		1611 Authorised Version of the Bible is published in England
		1616 Inigo Jones's Queen's House, Greenwich; William Shakespeare dies
		1618–48 Thirty Years War in Europe
		1619 Mortlake tapestry workshop is founded on the River Thames [10]
		1619–22 Inigo Jones's Banqueting House is built at Whitehall in London
1625–1649 Charles I		**1625**
		1626 Dutch settle at New Amsterdam (later New York) in America

	1627	Barbados Company founds first English colony in the West Indies
	1632	Anthony van Dyck becomes court painter to Charles I
	1634	Building of the Taj Mahal begins in Agra, India
	1637	First East India Company ship reaches Canton (Guangzhou) in China
	1639	Japan closes its ports to all countries except The Netherlands and China
	1640	Civil Wars begin in Scotland
	1641	Outbreak of the Irish Rebellion; John Evelyn begins his diary
	1642	Civil Wars begin in England
1649–1660 The Interregnum	**1649**	Execution of Charles I
	1650	
1654–1659 Oliver Cromwell,	**1651**	Charles II crowned King of Scots at Scone, then flees into exile
Lord Protector of England,	**1655**	English seize Jamaica from Spain
Scotland and Ireland	**1656**	Jews readmitted to England by Cromwell (expelled in 1290)
	1657	First English coffee shop opens in Oxford
1660–1685 Charles II	**1660**	Royal Society is founded in London; Samuel Pepys begins his diary
The Restoration [13]	**1663**	Drury Lane Theatre opens in London
	1665	Isaac Newton discovers gravity
	1665–7	Second Dutch War
	1666	Great Fire destroys much of London, including St Paul's cathedral
	1667	John Milton's poem *Paradise Lost* is published
	1668	English East India Company takes over Bombay (Mumbai)
	1672	John Dwight establishes a pottery at Fulham in London [12]
	1675	
	1675	Christopher Wren begins the rebuilding of St Paul's cathedral (finished 1709)
	1679	Ashmolean Museum is founded in Oxford
	1681	Charles II grants colony of Pennsylvania to William Penn
1685–1688 James II	**1685**	Louis XIV revokes the Edict of Nantes and 20,000 Huguenots subsequently arrive in England
1689–1702 William III	**1688**	The 'Glorious Revolution'
(William of Orange) and Mary	**1689**	William and Mary begin their rebuilding of Hampton Court and Kensington Palace [16]
II rule as joint monarchs		
Mary dies 1694; William	**1690**	James II is defeated by William III at the Battle of the Boyne
rules alone until 1702	**1699**	English ban imports of Indian painted cottons (chintz)
	1700	
1702–1714 Anne	**1702–13**	Britain is at war with France in the War of the Spanish Succession
	1707	Act of Union (England and Scotland) creates Great Britain; *The Tatler* is first published in London
	1713	Treaty of Utrecht confirms British possession of 13 American colonies and upper Canada
Reigns of the Hanoverian monarchs	**1715**	Colen Campbell's first volume of *Vitruvius Britannicus* is published
of Great Britain and Ireland	**1725**	
1714–1727 George I	**1725**	Lord Burlington begins to build Chiswick House in London [17]
	1729	China restricts European trade to the port of Canton (Guangzhou)
1727–1760 George II	**1731**	*The Gentleman's Magazine* is first published in London
	1738	Roubiliac's sculpture of Handel is erected in Vauxhall Gardens, London [20]; Herculaneum is excavated in Italy [22]
	1739–48	Britain and France at war in the War of the Austrian Succession
	1740	Samuel Richardson's novel *Pamela* is published
	1746	Jacobite army defeated by government forces at the Battle of Culloden

	1750	
	1752	Britain converts to the modern calendar; Francis Nixon begins plate-printing textiles in Ireland [24]
	1754	Thomas Chippendale's *Gentleman and Cabinet Maker's Director* is published [25]
	1756–63	Britain and France at war in the Seven Years War
	1757	East India Company takes control of Bengal in India
	1759	Carron ironworks is established in Scotland
1760–1820 George III	**1762**	James Stuart and Nicholas Revett publish *Antiquities of Athens* [22]
	1768	Royal Academy is established in London with Sir Joshua Reynolds as first President; Captain Cook begins his voyage to Australia and the Pacific; 'hard-paste' porcelain is made at Plymouth [19]
	1769	Josiah Wedgwood establishes his pottery at Etruria, Staffordshire [28]
	1771	Richard Arkwright sets up first cotton spinning mill in England
	1773–8	James and Robert Adam publish *Works in Architecture* [23]
	1775	
	1776	American Declaration of Independence leads to war with Britain
	1779	First iron bridge is erected at Coalbrookdale, Shropshire
	1783	War of American Independence ends; Britain recognises the United States of America
	1785	James Watt and Matthew Boulton install a steam engine in a cotton-spinning factory in Nottinghamshire
	1789	*Interesting Narrative of the Life of Olaudah Equiano* is published; French Revolution begins with the storming of the Bastille
	1791	First Catholic Relief Act allows Roman Catholics to worship freely in Britain for the first time since the Reformation [34]
	1792	Thomas Paine's *Rights of Man* and Mary Wollstonecraft's *Vindication of the Rights of Woman* are published
	1796	James Wyatt begins to build Fonthill Abbey for William Beckford [32]
	1798	Napoleon invades Egypt; British defeat the French at the Battle of the Nile
	1800	
	1800	Act of Union creates the political union of Great Britain and Ireland [29]
	1805	British defeat French and Spanish at the Battle of Trafalgar [29]
	1807	Thomas Hope's *Household Furniture and Interior Decoration* is published [30]
1811–1820 The Regency George III falls ill and his son, George, Prince of Wales, rules in his place as Regent [31]	**1811**	Luddites destroy machines in the north of England
	1813	Jane Austen's *Pride and Prejudice* is published
	1815	Napoleon is defeated at Waterloo
	1816	Jacquard loom is introduced to Britain [36]
	1818	Mary Shelley's *Frankenstein* is published
1820–1830 George IV	**1820**	First iron steamship is launched in Britain
	1825	
	1825	Stockton to Darlington Railway opens
1830–1837 William IV	**1829**	Catholic Emancipation Act allows Roman Catholics to sit in Parliament
	1832	Reform Act extends the vote in Britain
	1833	Slavery is abolished throughout the British Empire
	1835	First negative photograph taken by Henry Fox Talbot [37]
	1836	A.W.N. Pugin's *Contrasts* is published [34]

1837–1901 Victoria

1837–8	Charles Dickens's novel *Oliver Twist* is published
1840	Victoria marries Albert of Saxe-Coburg-Gotha [45]; Penny Postage is introduced in Britain; first Opium War between Britain and China
1840–7	New Palace of Westminster is built in the Gothic Revival style [33]
1841	Thomas Cook sells his first excursion ticket
1842	New laws are introduced to protect designs in Britain[41]; Treaty of Nanking confirms the British colony of Hong Kong; China opens new ports to outside trade
1845-7	Potato famine in Ireland leads to large-scale emigration
1845-9	Sikh Wars lead to British annexation of the Punjab in India
1848	Revolutions occur across Europe; Marx and Engels publish the *Communist Manifesto*
1850	
1851	Great Exhibition is held in the Crystal Palace in London [35]; John Ruskin's *Stones of Venice* is published; gold is found in Victoria, Australia
1852	Museum of Ornamental Art is founded, later called the South Kensington Museum, and then the Victoria and Albert Museum
1854-6	Crimean War, between Britain, France and Russia
1856	William Perkin discovers mauveine, the first synthetic dye [36]; Owen Jones's *Grammar of Ornament* is published
1857	Great Indian Rebellion (known as the Mutiny) begins; Science Museum is founded in South Kensington
1858	British Crown takes over control of India from the East India Company
1859	Charles Darwin's *Origin of Species* is published
1860	Second Opium War between China and Britain
1861	Death of Prince Albert [40]; William Morris establishes the firm Morris, Marshall, Faulkner & Co. [47]; first illustrated edition of Mrs Beeton's *Household Management* is published [46]; American Civil War begins; Kingdom of Italy is proclaimed
1871	Unification of Germany; Bank Holidays introduced in England and Wales
1874	First Impressionist exhibition opens in Paris
1875	
1876	Victoria is proclaimed Empress of India
1878	Electric street lighting is introduced in London
1882	Married Women's Property Act enables a married woman to have the same rights over property as an unmarried woman
1887	Victoria's Golden Jubilee
1888	Arts and Crafts Exhibition Society is established [48]
1896	Klondyke gold rush in Canada begins [44]
1897	Victoria's Diamond Jubilee; building of the Glasgow School of Art begins, designed by C.R. Mackintosh
1899	South Kensington Museum is renamed the Victoria and Albert Museum; Boer War breaks out in South Africa
1900	
1901	Death of Victoria

Practical Information

VICTORIA AND ALBERT MUSEUM
Cromwell Road, London SW7 2RL
Telephone: 020 7942 2000
Website: www.vam.ac.uk

RECORDED INFORMATION
General: 0870 442 0808
Current exhibitions: 0870 442 0809
Research facilities: 0870 442 0810
Branch museum information: 0870 442 0811

OPENING HOURS
Monday, Tuesday, Thursday to Sunday: 10.00–17.45
Wednesday: 10.00–22.00
Last Friday of every month: 10.00–22.00
Box office open Monday to Friday: 10.00–17.00
Telephone: 020 7942 2209

INFORMATION DESK
Staff will be happy to help with general queries concerning the collections or any other facilities at the Museum.

GUIDED TOURS
Free introductory tours, lasting about an hour, are available every day. Meet at the Cromwell Road entrance.

LEARNING AND VISITOR SERVICES
Gallery events, education programmes, and advice and assistance (before and during a visit).
Telephone: 020 7942 2197

THE PRINT ROOM
Open Tuesday to Friday: 10.00–16.30
Saturday: 10.00–13.00 and 14.30–16.30
Telephone: 020 7942 2563

THE NATIONAL ART LIBRARY
Open Tuesday to Saturday: 10.00–17.00
Enquiry service open Tuesday to Saturday: 10.00–17.00
Telephone: 020 7942 2400

OPINIONS SERVICE
First Tuesday of every month: 14.30–17.00
Free identification of works of art.

RESTAURANT
Telephone: 020 7942 2518
Monday to Sunday: 10.00–17.30
Late View candlelit dinners on Wednesdays: 18.30–21.30
Classical music on Sundays: 12.00–15.00

THE SHOPS
All three open daily: 10.00–17.45
In addition, the main shop is open late on Wednesday and Friday until 22.00
V&A shop online: www.vandashop.co.uk

FRIENDS OF THE V&A
Supporting the work of the Museum, the Friends give their time voluntarily as well as providing financial help. Benefits include discounts in the Museum shops, the restaurant and on V&A courses; free entry to exhibitions and special Friends events.
Friends office: 020 7942 2271
Friends membership desk: 020 7942 2280

ACKNOWLEDGEMENTS
I am very grateful to Gail Durbin, Sarah Medlam, Christopher Wilk, fellow members of the British Galleries Team and the following V&A staff for providing material for this book and offering help and advice: Julia Bigham, Clare Browne, Anthony Burton, Marian Campbell, Rachel Church, Frances Collard, Katie Coombs, Rosemary Crill, Judith Crouch, Ann Eatwell, Richard Edgcumbe, Rupert Faulkner, Simon Ford, Mark Haworth-Booth, Kate Hay, Robin Hildyard, Alun Graves, Reino Leifkes, Bet McCleod, Liz Miller, Tessa Murdoch, Charles Newton, Anthony North, Susan North, Linda Parry, Lucy Pratt, Michael Snodin, John Styles, Margaret Timmers, Marjorie Trusted, Rowan Watson, Ming Wilson, James Yorke, Hilary Young. I would also like to thank Jill & Edward Bace, Denise & Lauren Drake, Paul Harper, Maurice Howard, and Jill & Frances Winch for helpful comments on the text.

All photographs by the photographers of the V&A Photographic Studio: Pip Barnard, Richard Davis, Sara Hodges, Mike Kitcatt, Ken Jackson, Dominic Naish, Paul Robins, Christine Smith, Ian Thomas.

First published by V&A Publications 2001
© 2001 The Board of Trustees of the Victoria and Albert Museum

ISBN 1 85177 3622
Designed by Broadbase
Floor plans by Rose-Innes Associates
Printed in Italy